D1375756

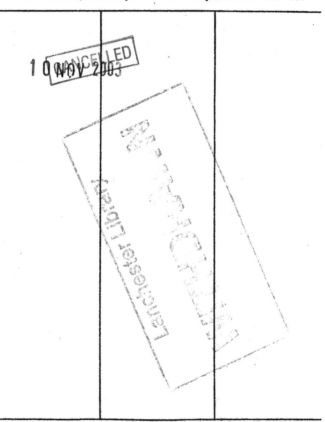

# Flute Technique

GARETH MORRIS

OXFORD UNIVERSITY PRESS

Oxford University Press is a department of the University of Oxford.
It furthers the University's objective of excellence in research, scholarship,
and education by publishing worldwide in

Oxford New York

Auckland Bangkok Buenos Aires Cape Town Chennai
Dar es Salaam Delhi Hong Kong Istanbul Karachi Kolkata
Kuala Lumpur Madrid Melbourne Mexico City Mumbai Nairobi
São Paulo Shanghai Taipei Tokyo Toronto

and associated companies in
Berlin Ibadan

Oxford is a trade mark of Oxford University Press

Published in the United States by
Oxford University Press Inc , New York

British Library Cataloguing in Publication Data
Data available

Library of Congress Cataloging in Publication Data
Morris, Gareth.
Flute technique / Gareth Morris.
Includes bibliographical references.
1 Flute—Instruction and study    I. Title.
MT 340.M73   1991
788.3'2193—dc20
ISBN 0-19-318432-X

Printed in Great Britain by Biddles Short Run Books, King's Lynn

# CONTENTS

# INTRODUCTION

THE finest flute sound, with a quality which can be greatly varied, both in dynamics and colour, must be built upon the sure foundations of tone, intonation, and purity of production; these qualities can only be acquired after diligent practice, for which a fine sense of pitch and a discerning ear are indispensable. Even these assets are not enough for the complete player, who must be a trained musician, with natural rhythm and a sensitive understanding of the music he hopes to interpret.

In order to prepare himself to be an artist it is therefore necessary for the beginner flautist to devote a great deal of time and patience to the study of the basic technique of controlling the instrument; it is to be his voice, whose sound will indicate the weaknesses which he hopes to eliminate and will release his feelings for the music, and the thoughts he had in preparing his interpretations.

It is unfortunate that many teachers of the flute, however well-meaning and enthusiastic, seem to be incapable of instructing their pupils in the correct way of blowing the instrument, with the result that bad habits accumulate alarmingly and can only be eradicated with great difficulty, and with the willing collaboration of teacher and student.

The object of this book is to place before the flautist the knowledge which will enable him to achieve the technique his natural talents need for the interpretation of music: the advice it contains is not for those who are more interested in the flute than in its repertoire, because its purpose is to help the player to perform in his own personal style, but with the control and discipline that are the essential equipment of the mature artist.

# THE HISTORY
# OF THE FLUTE

## A  The Old flute

### (i)  *The Development of the Baroque Instrument*

The origin of the flute is lost in the darkness of prehistory, so no actual person can be credited with its invention or discovery. It probably owes its existence to Pan; when Syrinx transformed herself into a reed to escape his attentions he plucked it and made a flute, to play his sorrows away. This prototype of all wind instruments consisted of a single tube which produced a musical sound when air was directed across its open end, and the next stage in its development was the addition of several shorter and longer pipes whose pitches formed a primitive scale. Later it was realized that the cutting of finger holes in the side of a single tube would enable the length of the vibrating air-column within to be varied, so that the same result was achieved in a much more manageable way. Pipes, blown at the end or across a mouth-hole bored in the side, have existed in India, China, Japan, Greece, and Egypt (where pictures of them and their players can be seen on the tombs of Pharaohs) from the earliest times, and such instruments played a prominent part in the cultural activities of all the ancient civilizations. With the collapse of the great Western Empires the flute seems to have disappeared, but it remained in the East, where it is played in its original form to this day—a bamboo tube with six finger-holes. Meanwhile the flute was silent, or at least neglected, in Europe until medieval times, when it reappeared as the recorder. This type of flute is blown through a mouthpiece at the end, like a whistle, and it became extremely popular in Germany and England, where it was made in several sizes, ranging from sopranino to a gigantic bass which had to rest on the floor. A complete set was known as a 'chest', and with viols, virginals, and madrigal consorts they were much used in performances of the superb music of the Elizabethan era, when English composers were the most distinguished in Europe. Nevertheless, music progressed, and the instruments had to follow suit: the English miniaturists epitomized by Dowland and Morley were succeeded by composers who needed a variety and subtlety of sound that earlier instruments lacked, so the viols became violins and cellos, the harpsichord displaced the clavichord and virginals, and the recorder surrendered to the transverse or side-blown flute, which was a superior instrument in volume and compass. The sound of the recorder is beautiful but its range of expression is limited, because it is the mouthpiece that determines the angle at which the airstream encounters the sound-hole. The player is therefore unable to alter the direction in order to adjust the pitch, which is affected by dynamics, so musical feelings have to be forgone in the cause of tolerable intonation. The transverse flute won the day, even at its seventeenth-century stage. Unfettered by a mouthpiece, the lips control the air without constraint and can exert much greater influence on tone and intonation; so with such a sophisticated instrument at their disposal the leading continental composers allowed its innocent predecessor to go into limbo, while they concentrated on a flute that could hold its own with the already powerful oboe and newly developed strings.

During most of the seventeenth century the flute was just a simple three-jointed wooden tube, stopped at the top end by a cork, with a hole for the mouth in the cylinder headjoint and six finger-holes in the conical body. The lowest note appeared when all the holes were closed, and as each finger was raised the other six notes of the scale followed. To obtain the second octave the process was repeated, with the lips slightly compressed to raise the direction of the air, and a third but shorter register was produced by reducing the size of the aperture, and using a system of cross-fingering. This was fairly satisfactory for playing in the key in which the flute was built—usually D major—but most of the semitones were obtained artificially, by closing holes lower down the tube, half-closing others and by turning the flute inwards or outwards. These adjustments had uneven results, so changes of key and chromatic passages presented difficulties which had to be overcome when Equal Temperament was superseding Just Intonation, and adventurous composers were no longer so restricted in their harmony. Bach composed his Forty-eight Preludes and Fugues to justify the new tuning, the whole spectrum of music was widening, and woodwind instruments had to accommodate to it. The next stage in flute construction was therefore directed at making the chromatic scale more accessible by adding holes for semitones, but progress was surprising slow; a D♯ hole with a closed key, opened by the right-hand little finger, was the only addition to the simple flute which served Bach and his contemporaries and was the standard instrument of the brilliant Baroque Period. Its leading exponent was Quantz, and his famous pupil Frederick the Great was perhaps the doyen of all the enthusiastic and gifted amateurs to whom the development of the flute owes so much; but only in the hands of a master was it good enough for Mozart.

## (ii) The Flute in the Late Eighteenth and Early Nineteenth Centuries

Mozart's well-documented dislike of the flute should not be regarded as his dismissal of the instrument, but rather as an acute sensitivity to its weaknesses: he greatly appreciated the beauty and extraordinary variety of emotions that a sound of apparent simplicity contained. Warmth, pathos, charm, and even heroism are all manifest in Mozart's flute music, but very few players of those one-keyed eighteenth-century instruments were able to satisfy his unique ear for intonation. 'Every time one must be anxious whether the expected tone is too low or too high,' he declared, and even the flautists agreed. He accepted commissions for concertos from rich amateurs because money was needed, but only after hearing J. B. Wendling of the famous Mannheim orchestra did he really welcome the flute, and elevate it to the prominent position that it enjoys in his later scores. 'His heart, his ears, and the tip of his tongue are in the right place,' he said of that artist—surely one of the most impressive citations in musical history. It was patently urgent that this important instrument should be succoured, and flute makers were diligent in the last years of that century; extra holes for semitones appeared, with keys to be opened by disengaged fingers, so that chromatic passages were simplified; the compass was extended by a tone, down to C♮; and the power and clarity of the highest register benefited from these additions; but intonation remained the bane of the flautist's life because the holes had to be bored in acoustically incorrect positions if they were to be within reach of the fingers. Notwithstanding its defects this eight-keyed flute enjoyed immense success among amateurs, and interesting professional players emerged in the first decades of the nineteenth century. A succession of flautist-composers flourished in England and abroad—virtuosi who performed technical feats, usually of their own creation, before admiring audiences of enthusiasts who often engaged the celebrities to give them lessons. Variations on popular airs were the fashion, so there was ample opportunity for the *aficionados* to consider who could play the greater number of staccato notes in a bar, which artist produced the more affecting tone in an Adagio, or whose trills were the most even and delicate in the midst of such artistry. Many of them made an excellent livelihood, augmenting their incomes by publishing compositions and instruction books, but the most prosperous of the English players was Charles Nicholson (1795–1837), first professor of the flute in the Royal Academy of Music, whose alterations to his instrument were the inspiration for the revolutionary change in flute design which came later in the nineteenth century. Nicholson was a brilliant performer whose excellent ear, strong lip muscles, and large hands enabled him to use a flute of his own specifications which would have been unmanageable for most players. His enlargement of the finger and mouth-holes resulted in a stronger sound and more flexibility of pitch, but made great demands on the embouchure, and needed the imperious authority of a musician of his calibre. This was the state of the flute when in 1831 the celebrated Theobald Boehm of Munich arrived in London to give recitals. He heard Nicholson play, and was so impressed by the grandeur of his tone that he decided to embark upon the design of a completely new model.

In August 1871 he wrote to the London flautist W. S. Broadwood, 'I did as well as any Continental flautist in London in 1831, but I could not match Nicholson in power of tone, wherefore I set to work to remodel my flute. Had I not heard him, probably the Boehm flute would never have been made.'

## B The New Flute: Theobald Boehm

### (i) *His Experiments and First Improvements*

Theobald Boehm (1794–1881) was a distinguished flautist who showed musical gifts as a boy, and quite naturally absorbed his father's skills as a goldsmith while still studying the flute; indeed he practised both professions for several years, until in 1818 he was appointed flautist of the orchestra in Munich. He possessed a scientifically inventive mind, and having constructed his own instruments he later established a flute-making business, while he still pursued a successful playing career that led to his London visit. Boehm's astonishment at the power and variety of Nicholson's performances, and the sight of the flute that gave such a majestic sound, convinced him that an entirely new design was necessary, with larger holes whose positions would depend on pitch rather than the size of the hands—and no time was spared in starting his experiments. His new flute appeared in 1832, with significant alterations which heralded the much greater transformation that was to come. Larger holes released more tone and could still be covered by normal fingers, and better venting for the sound was provided by a reversal of the positions of the semitone keys; these were now normally open, and could be closed by simple mechanism connecting them to rings under the fingers, which depressed them while covering their own holes. This instrument represents the first step from the baroque and classical flutes to the one in use today, and it inspired its creator to continue his improvements in an even more dramatic style.

## (ii) *The Final 1847 Model*

Boehm's flute of 1832 did not achieve an immediate success, because its very superiority made great demands upon the application of the average player. The new arrangement of the keys was confusing; a larger mouth-hole provided more sound and greater opportunity to direct the intonation, but it needed stronger breath and lip control, and the size and position of the tone-holes remained problematical; only the professionals had the time and the skill to appreciate the significance of the improvements, and they demonstrated the instrument's powers to such good effect that in a few years it was almost universally acclaimed. Nevertheless, Boehm himself knew that his flute was still imperfect; he was also aware that his knowledge of acoustics was inadequate for more advanced experiments, so he embarked upon an intensive study of the subject in order to construct an instrument which would be so excellent that players would be able to concentrate entirely on eliminating their own faults.

After research at the University of Munich he came to the conclusion that the bore of the whole tube would have to be radically altered. The sound of every other wind instrument is generated at its smaller end, so Boehm saw no reason why this should not apply to the flute, and after much thought and many experiments he gave this final model a cylindrical body and a headjoint which tapered, in an almost parabolic curve, towards the mouth-hole. There was no longer any hesitation with regard to the deployment of the tone-holes; their correct positions were mathematically calculated, they were so large that only keys could cover them, and then an elegant system of mechanism was devised so that nine fingers were able to open and close fifteen holes without difficulty.

The culmination of years of concentration was a triumph; in 1847 Boehm's ingenuity and persistence brought forth a virtually faultless instrument. The new bore gave a powerful sound which could be reduced to pianissimo; the internal dimensions of the headjoint ensured that the three registers were equally focused, and the accurate placing of large tone-holes allowed an unprecedented command of intonation and dynamics. The great Cremonese violin makers of earlier centuries brought their art to a supremacy that remains unchallenged, but a beautiful instrument depends upon its player: in a similar manner Theobald Boehm disposed of the faults that had caused such frustration to those who were aware of them, but he created a flute that needed the control of a master for it to be heard to its greatest advantage.

### (iii) *Later Modifications and Additions*

Boehm's masterpiece was unreservedly applauded by the best flautists, and remains the definitive flute throughout the world; yet there were players whose own inadequacies inspired useful, but inessential, additions and minor alterations to the standard model. Boehm would have accepted some of them, but attempts to simplify flute-playing usually disturbed his carefully considered schema, and they were often his own discarded ideas. Nevertheless, enthusiasm for accessories and modifications was not ephemeral, and a small number of them have become regular component parts of the mechanism. Briccialdi, an Italian flautist, invented an improved B♭ device that is now in universal use; Dorus, in France, devised a closed G♯ key to accommodate players who were inexplicably confused by Boehm's superior open version, and this has unfortunately prevailed; and the English players Rockstro and Brossa both patented levers in order to reduce the element of peril inherent in the highest F♯, and which can also dispose of certain fingering problems in passages involving this note in all three registers. The French makers have almost reverted to the old ring system by perforating the centres of five keys, a variation which has attracted many devotees who have difficulty in giving reasons for their conversion; numerous shapes and sizes of mouth-hole have been tested and discarded; and there are perennial arguments about the materials of which the flute should be constructed, but not many ideas of real consequence have materialized since the appearance of 'The Celebrated Cylindric Bore Boehm's Improved System Concert Flute' in 1847.

# 2

# THE TECHNIQUE OF
# PLAYING THE FLUTE

## A The Acoustics of the Instrument

Every sound, made by bells, strings, or vibrating columns of air, is composed of a fundamental tone with an infinite number of higher notes resulting from it; these overtones contribute to the resonance, are not usually heard independently, and form a natural phenomenon which is known as the Harmonic Series. In the playing of wind instruments the notes in this series are separated, by a method of blowing which is explained later; this technique is necessary for playing nearly every note on brass instruments, but it is used on the flute only to produce its various registers, and so obtain a compass of more than three octaves from a tube of only 26½ inches in length.

Sections B (ii) and (iii) of this chapter contain instructions for achieving this, but the student must first be made aware of the nature of the sounds he hopes to control. Like the movements of the planets, the Harmonic Series can be mathematically plotted. The first of the resultant tones becomes the second rung of the harmonic ladder, and is stationed precisely one octave above the fundamental, or first, harmonic; the next interval is a fifth; then a fourth, followed by major and minor thirds, until at the eighth harmonic the pitch is three octaves above, and the notes are so close together that a scale appears. These higher members of the series are used by brass players, but the flautist only takes advantage of the first (fundamental) and the second, until certain others are employed in the third register.

The shorter the tube, the higher the note. The most primitive form of flute consisted of a number of pipes bound together in order of size, and therefore of pitch; but later

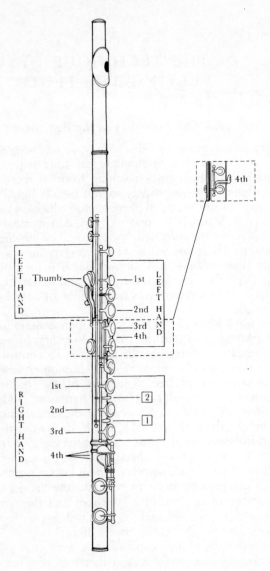

Figure 1

came the discovery that the same result could be obtained from a single tube, with side holes covered by the fingers. The lowest note sounded when they were all closed; as each was opened the air column became shorter, and the pitch was higher. This is the principle upon which the modern flute is constructed, as were the instruments of the seventeenth and eighteenth centuries which are discussed in the first chapter.

## B First principles

### (i) Assembling the Parts of the Flute

Before embarking upon the long and fascinating journey from the beginning of flute-playing to the demanding thrills of actually performing, it is essential that the student should set himself the highest standards of behaviour to his instrument. First he must learn to put it together correctly, and realize that it is of great importance that the several parts are always placed in exactly the same position with regard to each other.

The flute consists of three joints; the headjoint, in which is bored the mouth-hole and which is stopped at one end by an adjustable cork (see Section D (ii)); the body, with its apparently complicated mechanism; and the footjoint, which has three, and sometimes four, keys.

These three parts are easily assembled to make the complete flute, by fitting them into each other and then twisting them, so that the mouth-hole is in a straight line with the centre of the main keys of the body, as is the rod (or axle) on the footjoint.

The instrument is now so arranged that when correctly placed upon the lower lip, and the air blown across the mouth-hole in the right direction, it will respond to a player whose physical equipment is normal; most people have no problems.

### (ii) Fingering and Sound Production of the First Register

The sound of any wind instrument is produced by blowing a sensitively controlled stream of air into it; and the formation of the lips which is necessary for this is known as the embouchure, as is the part of the instrument to which it is applied.

In the case of the flute the embouchure is the mouth-hole of the headjoint, across which the player directs the air in such a way that it encounters the opposite side, setting in vibration the air column within the tube. This must be achieved with the minimum of waste, although half the air will escape.

The method of doing this is surprisingly simple, and yet it can be all too easily mismanaged: unhealthy habits make their insidious way into the embouchure and can powerfully resist the attempts of the inexperienced player, and often confuse the incompetent teacher.

To make certain that all will be well, it is wise to avoid indulging in experiments that are so frequently recommended; it is dangerous to turn the hole this way and that, to try one lip position and another, or to be influenced by what seems to be the least objectionable of the sounds that first appear.

Pitch is more important than tone, especially at the beginning, and true intonation will produce the most beautiful results in the end (see Section D of this chapter).

Using the headjoint alone, the student places the inner edge of the mouth-hole on the bottom of the lower lip so that it is very slightly turned inwards, enabling the air-stream to hit the opposite side. The lip should project over one third of the hole and the mouth must be nearly closed, the corners being drawn back in a slight smile, so that the lips rest firmly against the upper and lower teeth, without any undue strain. Then, after a deep breath, the beginner blows, with strength and confidence, pronouncing the syllable 'tu', as in French. At this point the first sound that has any recognizable pitch will be a wild Ab, because most headjoints are of the length which produces that note; however ugly it is, it nevertheless indicates that the flute may now be assembled, and studies are about to start in earnest.

The mechanism that closes the holes in the body and footjoint of the flute was invented by Theobald Boehm in the early nineteenth century (see Chapter 1, Section B (i)), when he realized that the unsatisfactory intonation of the instrument would remain almost impossible to correct while those holes remained within reach of the fingers. What appears to be a formidable array of complicated machinery is only a means of simplifying the fingering, and making it possible to play with almost equal facility in all keys; so it is of the utmost importance that the flautist should take advantage of Boehm's innovations by using only the correct fingerings, unless an alternative is absolutely necessary.

Placing the fingers on the keys demands careful thought and practice, because three of them are involved in supporting the instrument. The flute rests against the lower lip, with gentle pressure from the top joint of the left-hand first finger, but it is properly held in position by the right-hand thumb and little finger. Those two are positioned, respectively, beneath the instrument (directly below the first finger), and above it (lightly pressing downwards on the lever of the opened D♯ key), and it should be quite easy to balance the flute in this way, so that the other fingers of each hand are unstrained; when the D♯ is closed, the other fingers are in use and can complement the thumb. A stiff left hand causes undue pressure of the flute against the first finger, and it also hinders the thumb's comfortable manipulation of its double key—indeed that thumb exerts a critical influence upon the position of the hand. When it is at the correct angle, i.e. sideways between the two levers, every finger falls into place naturally; but in a flat state it has to slide from one lever to the other, instead of turning, and the hand is pulled from its correct contact with the mechanism, which is beautifully designed to accommodate the slightly curved fingers. Practice will confirm that they fit perfectly on to the keys when they are correctly arranged, and concentration on the acquisition of a healthy technique will be made easier.

The normal compass of the flute is considered to be three octaves (Middle C ($C^1$) to $C^4$), the two higher of which are obtained by producing harmonics from the lowest, or fundamental.

**Chart 1.**    Normal fingering of the first register

*Note:* (a) the D♯ lever MUST be depressed, so that its key is open, for ALL notes in this register except C♮¹ C♯¹ D♭¹ D♮²;

     (b) the first finger of the left hand MUST be lifted for D♮².

     (c) A and B are interchangeable fingerings for the two notes, and the choice of fingering depends on context.

● Finger down
○ Finger up

Having studied the chart for that register the student now attempts to play B♭: this is the most suitable starting note because its sounding hole is in the centre of the tube and it is consequently one of the most stable in that octave. With the lower lip covering one third of the mouth-hole, which is very slightly turned in, the air is blown across it so that it is split by the outer edge, thus sending one half into the flute and the other half over it. If the air is directed across the room, at an object which is just below the level of the embouchure, the required B♭ will result, and the beginner will be able to produce its neighbours in that octave without any change of lip position; it should be noted that if there is no variation in the dynamics the same embouchure will obtain all the notes in the lowest octave, and they will be in tune. This must be attempted immediately an acceptable B♭ is sounded.

The fundamental notes range from $C^1$ to $C\sharp^2$, and it is important to realize that this last one is not, as is generally thought, sharp in pitch and difficult to control: when produced in exactly the same way as our original example, $B\flat^1$, it is as firm and accurate as any other.

It is strongly recommended that at this stage an *mf* dynamic is used, because when the flute is played *f* the pitch rises, and the opposite in *p*: this crucial facet of flute technique is to be approached later, indeed only when the initial difficulties of sound production have been overcome.

Flute tone and the pure intonation that influences it are of greater importance than the acquisition of finger dexterity, on which so many flautists concentrate: even at this elementary stage quite rapid passages appear to be surprisingly easy, and many innocent parents are led to believe that their child is a genius. Often the student has progressed much further before he realizes that the fatal facility of this marvellous instrument is extremely difficult to control, and that the complicated and often rapid passages demanded by composers can only be negotiated after the long and patient practice of scales and exercises in all keys, and with the most varied of dynamics and articulations.

Chart 2.    Normal fingering of the second register

*Note:* (a) the D♯ lever MUST be depressed, so that its key is open, for all notes in the second register;
(b) the first finger of the left hand MUST be raised for D♯² (E♭²).
(c) A and B are interchangeable fingerings for the two notes, and the choice of fingering depends on context.

### (iii) *Fingering and Sound Production of the Second and Third Registers*

Having attained some command of the lower notes the study of the second octave can now be discussed. These sounds are harmonics, and they are obtained from the lower register, using the same fingering but increasing the speed of the air-stream; this is not done by blowing harder but by reducing the size of the embouchure and raising the direction of the air. The lower lip is slightly protruded so that the air is now directed at an object which is just *higher* than the embouchure; this procedure not only reduces the size of the slit between the lips, but also raises the jet of air, thus producing the second register, bounded by $D\natural^2$ and $C\sharp^3$. However, the first of these notes ($D\natural^2$) is abnormal, in that no change of lip position is necessary; the first finger of the left hand (see fingering chart) is lifted to open a hole which acts as a vent, automatically raising the note by a perfect octave. The same finger is also used for $D\sharp^2$, but here the embouchure is moved to the second octave position, to correct what would otherwise be a flat note. It will now be apparent that if $D\natural^2$ is blown with a low register embouchure and $D\sharp^2$ as in the second octave, their intonation will be perfect without any unnatural adjustments.

Just as Bb is recommended as a suitable note for the initial practice of the first octave, so $G\natural^2$ has been found to be the safest one to use when attempting work on the second, or middle, register (see Section A of this chapter for an explanation of the Harmonic Series).

An exercise to facilitate the correct production of these two octaves makes use of the interval $Bb^1/G\natural^2$; the direction of the air-stream for $G\natural$ must be at the same angle *above* level as it is *below* for Bb, and the notes are to be practised legato and *mf* until the lower lip moves smoothly forward and back again.

The player will quickly sense that he is controlling the sound *and* the pitch; indeed the intonation will indicate whether or not the sound is being properly produced. At this

Chart 3.   Normal fingering of the third register

*Note:* (a) the D♯ lever MUST be depressed for ALL notes in the third register *except* B♭³, B♮³ and C♮⁴. It is essential that the key remains closed for these three notes, although they are obtainable when it is open.

(b) A and B are interchangeable fingerings for the two notes, and the choice of fingering depends on context.

stage the G♮ is often too flat for the B♭, and its correction by means of a further projection of the lower lip will automatically bring the tone into focus.

It will now be clear that tone and pitch are dependent upon each other. The possession of a tuning fork (A = 440) is vital, and a naturally good ear is indispensable. If the position of the adjustable cork in the headjoint is incorrect (see Section D (ii)) none of these instructions will be effective, so it is never to be moved after it has been accurately set.

The forward embouchure that has been discussed controls the notes between D$\sharp^2$ and C$\sharp^3$ inclusive, and produces the second harmonic in the series which has been explained in Section A of this chapter. The player is advised to work on these notes firmly and bravely, with a *mf* dynamic, until he is confident that he is able to play them with a pure, strong sound; no attempt should be made to practise loudly or softly until Sections D and F of this chapter have been studied.

The third register starts on D♮$^3$, and it appears to involve an alarming combination of fingerings; the novice will imagine that such high notes require more breath, a firmer pressure of the lips, and a still higher direction of the air-stream, but correct methods and an understanding of the fingering system will show that he need have little fear.

The production of these harmonics is in fact assisted by the opening of certain tone-holes in the upper part of the tube, thus enabling the register to be obtained without any significant effort—provided that the second octave is blown correctly.

It will be observed that, with the exception of the first note (D♮$^3$), the fingerings until G♮$^3$ are identical to those of the fundamental octave, but with the addition of one opened hole in the left hand which acts as a vent; e.g. E♭$^3$ is fingered in the same way as E♭$^1$, with the G$\sharp$ key depressed; and in each case the vent-hole is situated a perfect fourth above its master. Careful study of the chart will now reveal that the fingering is considerably less complicated than it appears to be, and the embouchure will almost imperceptibly adapt itself to provide a necessary smaller outlet for the air-stream.

A simple method of preparing for the exploration of this new flute region is to play a firm $F\natural^2$, ensuring that it is blown in exactly the right direction, and then lift the middle finger of the left hand; this will open the $B\flat$ hole, in its capacity as a vent, and $F\natural^3$ will introduce itself with very little resistance. A minute upward movement of the lip will have reduced the size of the embouchure, and there will be surprise and relief that such an altitude has been achieved with so little effort.

The regular practice of this simple exercise will be of great help in acquiring mastery of the highest reaches of the instrument.

It was indicated in Section B (ii) of this chapter that the syllable 'tu' is to be pronounced when articulating every note on the flute, and indeed on all wind instruments. Obviously this does not apply to those within slurred phrases, but it is stressed that it is not just a beginner's technique or one for any particular register. Students are often careless and are inclined to take short cuts, so immediate insistence on the highest standards will have beneficial and lasting results; a note produced without articulation will be uncontrolled because the embouchure is unformed at the outset, therefore care in tonguing when practising the high notes will ensure that the sound is pure.

The necessary minute movement of the lip which was demonstrated in the leap from $F^2$ to $F^3$ conveniently encourages the tongue to work slightly closer to the top front teeth; but it must never touch them, and on no account is to be allowed to protrude between the lips.

Some of the high notes have characteristics which will be discussed later (see Chapter 3, Section D), but they are not particularly difficult to obtain; having reached the top octave by way of $F^2$ and $F^3$ it is advisable to practise the ascending and descending chromatic scale from $D\natural^3$ to $C\natural^4$. This must be done very slowly, using only the preferred fingerings, and the flute is to remain in one position throughout the exercise (see B (ii)). Temptation to turn it in or out is to be resisted; it is the function of the *lips* to direct operations, so any change in the placing of the mouth-hole will result in uncertainty, and the indiscriminate indulgence of experiments (see B (ii) paragraph 4).

The student is to use only the fingerings in Charts 1, 2, and 3 until he is able to play scales in all keys. He is then entitled to consult those given in Chapter 3.

## C   Breath Control

Breathing, a ceaseless activity, would appear to be the simplest feature of flute technique; but singers and wind players have to use their lungs for additional purposes, necessitating control of the air-stream in slightly unnatural ways. It is useful to know exactly what is done. 'Take a breath and blow' would be the suggestion of many a fine artist; however, long experience does not always indicate knowledge of the bad habits that so often beset the beginner. Faults in breathing can be difficult to eradicate, so it is vital that students should understand that such simple yet perfectly correct advice can only be useful after further guidance.

The ordinary person is not used to breathing really deeply. Flautists ensure that their lungs are completely filled when they take a breath; some doctors consider that professional players develop the capacity for breathing in great depth even when they are not blowing an instrument, and it is known that this can contribute to excellent health, after much experience and with daily practice.

Although the lungs are inflated in order to send the air into the flute, the pressure to expel it comes from the diaphragm, situated just beneath them. Breaths are therefore taken in, and exhaled, by using that muscle, in conjunction with the lower ribs. The flautist stands or sits in a perfectly upright position, with the chest held high and the shoulders remaining low and relaxed; any tension will impede access of air to the lungs, making control difficult and so producing a thin strangulated sound.

With these thoughts in mind it is safe to take a deep breath and blow; and at this point the abdominal muscles are used in conjunction with the embouchure, which plays a critical part in controlling the intensity of the air-stream and its destiny.

Wind players have known for centuries that beauty of tone, pure intonation and the singing qualities of their instruments can be cultivated only by the assiduous practice of long notes. The sound is held for as long as possible, starting quietly, continuing with crescendo and diminuendo, and then dying away to nothing. This exercise will be useless unless the pitch remains constant, and the quality of tone is always pure: control of intonation is considered in Section D of this chapter, and the actual production of the notes has been dealt with in Section B (ii) and (iii), but it is also essential to understand the reasons for taking breath at specific places in the music, and not at others. A true sense of rhythm is necessary for relaxed breathing, because the pulse of a phrase indicates the moment to inhale; and in the same way, a sensitive musician feels instinctively when the air is to be released.

Everyday breathing is natural and regular: the flautist's apparently unusual way of doing it becomes easy and unconscious when it is synchronized with the music. It follows that the daily practice of scales is one of the most beneficial disciplines for the improvement of breathing in wind-playing.

In strict time, musically phrased, and with appropriate accents, scales in all keys will help to develop the use of the abdominal muscles for drawing in a large quantity of air quickly, and expelling it slowly.

## D   Intonation

### (i) *Embouchure Control*

Mozart disliked the flute because it was so rarely played in tune. Nevertheless, he reluctantly created musical gems for the many rich and influential dilettanti of the instrument: he needed money, and one hopes he escaped the ordeal of listening to their efforts. Enthusiastic amateurs of the eighteenth century were not seriously concerned with niceties of pitch or subtleties of nuance, but some of the formidable professional virtuosi who appeared during later decades were anxious to make improvements to the flute. Several of them tried to do this by adding keys, others attempted to disguise its faults by the sheer power of their playing, but nothing really succeeded until Theobald Boehm designed his entirely new system of fingering, which enabled the holes to be placed in their correct acoustical positions (see Chapter 1, Section B (ii)).

The modern flute is perhaps the most perfect woodwind instrument; it can be played beautifully in tune by fine artists, yet the command of intonation remains one of its great challenges and can only be achieved with knowledge, practice, and a fine ear.

The problem lies in the fact that the pitch rises in crescendo, and descends in diminuendo, unless it is corrected; indeed playing would be much easier if dynamics and accents could be ignored.

Directions for blowing the flute in Sections B (ii) and (iii) of this chapter provide only for a mezzo-forte sound, so before considering the control of intonation over a wide range of tone it is necessary to be confident that embouchure positions are correct in the various registers. Playing with expression, with musical phrasing, and with accented rhythms, entails a mastery of embouchure control which has to be directed by the ear. 'Your ears will always lead you right, but you must know why,' said Anton Webern; but in flute-playing you must also know how.

The student will now be aware that fluctuations in pitch are hindering his attempts to vary the dynamics, and he will discover that lip control is necessary to counteract them. Playing a loud note with a long diminuendo involves the use of less and less breath, and this causes flattening of the pitch if it is not checked at the same time. Stability is achieved by a very small forward movement of the lower lip, a change of embouchure which raises the air-stream and reduces the size of the aperture. The amount of adjustment can only be decided by the ear; technical knowledge is useless if hearing is defective, so constant, critical listening must become habitual. The difference in direction is minute, and it changes exactly with the decrease in air-pressure, so the process becomes automatic after regular and discerning practice. Precisely the opposite technique is used in crescendo; the lips are constantly controlling the intonation as the pressure varies, so the character of the sound is greatly influenced by their partnership with the lungs and abdominal muscles.

Practising sound production in the flute's three registers will have already made much of this technique familiar, but the student is now progressing towards a more delicate use of the embouchure to which there is no short cut. It is absolutely essential that the original positions of the mouth are correct before proceeding with these exercises; there are to be no extra experiments in the placing of the mouth-hole; the flute remains in the proper position and must not be moved in order to influence pitch or dynamics. Moving from one octave to another obviously involves similar but larger changes in the embouchure; the smaller movements are contained in the greater.

A mistaken supposition is that an intrinsic weakness in the flute causes flat low notes and a sharp top octave, but when this occurs it is invariably the fault of the player.

A well-made instrument, correctly blown, will give true octaves throughout its compass, so students should be forbidden to make alterations to the measurements, or to tamper with the headjoint cork after this has been properly set.

Many beginners produce a flat fundamental register, having discovered that it is easier to play when the air is directed towards the hole instead of across it (see B (ii)). This bad habit enlarges the interval between the low notes and the less pliable top octave, an area which is often forced into ugly sharpness by inexperienced flautists. Strenuous exertion and tight lips injure high notes; those sounds consist of assisted harmonics which come easily with a small relaxed aperture, an embouchure that ensures stable intonation if the tone is pure. However, it is not to be assumed that intonation in the third octave can be controlled by relaxation; the notes are obtainable without undue effort, but a secure unforced embouchure is needed to ensure that the pitch remains constant amidst a variety of dynamics and changes of tone. In forte and crescendo passages the mouth is held firm by its corners, and the lower lip is very slightly withdrawn so that the pitch does not rise; with this knowledge, and with regular practice, the flute can be blown very hard without there being any distortion of the sound or sharpness of pitch. In quiet playing, and in diminuendo, the muscles of the mouth are used similarly, without any strain, and a forward position of the lower lip supports the intonation.

The normal dimensions of a flute require that it should be flattened when warmth has made the pitch rise. This is done by slightly withdrawing the headjoint; its tenon is also a tuning slide. If the adjustment is not made, and a flat low octave will certainly not encourage it, even unforced high notes will inevitably be sharp.

### (ii) The Cork in the Headjoint

The position of the headjoint cork, or stopper, is of critical importance. Its influence is such that the intonation of the whole instrument is dramatically disturbed if it is improperly placed; the truth of the three octaves and even the scale intervals are seriously affected by the slightest change in its distance from the centre of the mouth-hole.

Playing in tune becomes mysteriously difficult when the flute is maladjusted at the point where the sound is generated, and the production of a free tone can be an effort or is sometimes too easy, depending on the direction in which the cork is wrongly set.

Teachers are often unable to diagnose the condition, and they are inclined to encourage pupils to make experiments that can exacerbate the problems rather than solve them; the player strives to control pitch and tone, an unhealthy embouchure develops, and practising becomes a struggle instead of a pleasure unless the cause of the difficulties is quickly detected.

Ignorance of the effect the cork can have upon the acoustics of the flute leads to many an unnecessary change of headjoint; some flautists ill-advisedly dispose of excellent instruments and buy supposedly superior ones, without realizing that a small adjustment could end their frustration and enable them to progress naturally.

The distance from the end of the cork to the centre of the embouchure hole ought to be 17 mm., which is also the diameter of the bore of the quasi-parabolic headjoint at that point: if the diameter is correct, and also that of the 19 mm. cylindrical body of the flute, then the cork may be placed in that position, and the intonation will be true unless it is improperly produced.

Unfortunately it is usually necessary for the cork to be slightly moved, unless it has been set by an expert who is aware of its function and can blow the flute with authority.

The following reasons for this should be known before the cork can be adjusted with confidence.

(1) The cork may have been carelessly set

Makers use a measuring rod, with a mark 17mm. from one end, which is inserted into the headjoint. If the cork is in the right place the mark appears in the centre of the mouth-hole. This vague method is unreliable for determining the exact measurement; the cork is part of an instrument that is constructed to the highest degree of accuracy, and the crafts-man's eye cannot establish its precise position. The final arbiter must be the ear of an experienced flautist.

(2) The diameter of the bore at the centre of the mouth-hole may be incorrect

An adjustment of the cork can compensate for a *small* inaccuracy. Since 1945 flute makers have been attempting to improve upon the instrument designed with great precision by Theobald Boehm, who was uniquely qualified in music and the science of acoustics. The object has been to make flute-playing easier for thousands of enthusiastic customers, and an enlargement of the bore at the top of the headjoint has this effect, particularly upon the lower octave; but any alteration to the measurements, made in order to facilitate sound production, disturbs the intonation and upsets the higher registers.

A master-player is able to place the cork in its correct position without using a gauge, provided that he is fully cognizant of the influence that the slightest movement has upon the acoustics. The consequences are listed below ((*a*) and (*b*)) but such knowledge is precarious for those who are not absolutely sure of embouchure technique, and whose ear is not true.

It is wise to start by checking that the cork is roughly in the right place, by means of the mark which is to be found on most cleaning rods, and the following information will indicate how it can be finally set so that the sound is perfectly focused.

(a)  Cork positioned more than 17mm. from the mouth-hole
        centre

This draws the three octaves towards each other, and distorts their scales. The *lowest register* is unevenly sharpened, with some notes less affected than others. The left-hand C♯ and C♮ are slightly flattened, so the uninitiated will imagine that they have been improved; downwards from B♮ the notes become too sharp, and again the inexperienced will consider that they are easier to play. The *middle register* is similarly uneven, but flat, and its production is made difficult. The left-hand notes are the most affected, but the scale of the right hand is more distorted; F♯ and F♮ are flat, whereas E♮, E♭ and D♮ are surprisingly sharp. The *third register* is rigidly flat and unresponsive, with the exception of D♯ and F♯, which are easy to produce but sharp in pitch.

(b)  Cork positioned less than 17mm. from the mouth-hole
        centre

Ease of production when the cork is too near the embouchure often engenders the belief that it is then in its best position;

the temptation to enjoy this, and to ignore the impure intonation it causes, must be resisted. In most respects the results are the opposite to those discussed in paragraph (a), and it is just as necessary to be aware of them. The tone of the *lowest octave* is misleadingly good, but its average pitch is lowered, although C♯² and C♮² are very sharp; from B♮ downwards the notes are flat, and they are slow to respond when articulated. In the *middle register* an essential resistance is removed by the reduction of the space between the stopper and the mouth-hole. Students who find this is a comfortable way of playing are apparently unaware that most of the octave is sharp when the flute is subjected to such an imbalance; however, the flatness of E♮, E♭, and D♯ in the right hand should be a warning that the acoustics have been disturbed. E♮ is the worst affected of these flat notes, and because the cork is often placed in this wrong position it shares with the sharpened C♯² an undeserved reputation for being out of tune; both notes are excellent when the instrument is properly regulated (see B (ii) and (iii)).

The *third register* also becomes too easy to produce, and encourages a sweet tone that can beguile the innocent player into imagining that the cork is in its ideal position. Quiet playing is not difficult, but greater dynamics become uncontrollable; the entire octave is sharp except F♯³ and D♯³, whose apparently good qualities are deceptive (see B (ii) and (iii)).

This information also applies when the bore of the headjoint is inaccurate (see (2) of this section). If the bore is too *large* the symptoms are similar to those listed in (b); the cork must therefore be moved minutely away from the embouchure until the various faults are eliminated, but not far enough to allow those described in (a) to replace them. When the bore is too *small*, a rare occurrence, the process is reversed: the faults will be those listed in (a), so the cork is moved towards the mouth-hole until they are cured, but without allowing those in (b) to emerge. Adjustment of the cork involves turning the button at the top of the headjoint. It should be screwed in a clockwise direction to move it outwards; and anti-clockwise, and pushed in, to do the opposite.

## E   The Tongue

In wind-playing the tongue and the air-stream resemble consonants and vowels, whereas on stringed instruments the bow does duty for them both: the function of the tongue is to launch the sound, and then influence much of the phrasing by subtle articulation.

In Section B (iii) it is stated that all notes, except those with a slur, *must* be initiated by the tongue; its use gives the sound a clear beginning, affects the position of the embouchure and hence the direction of the air.

The tongue remains invisible in all circumstances; its appearance between the lips indicates a vulgar style, causes an unclear articulation and disturbs the embouchure, so students should be restrained from indulging this easily acquired habit. The tongue remains relaxed when it is not in use, its owner being almost unaware of its presence, but while working as an instrument of precision its position is very important. On pronouncing the syllable 'tu' at the beginning of a note (never 'ter', 'too', or 'te', because they distort the embouchure) the tongue will find its correct point of contact with the palate. This is immediately behind the top teeth, without touching them, but the necessary embouchure adjustments for the various registers will influence its position, so that it will be minutely closer to the teeth for the high notes and slightly further back for the low ones. Tonguing in the low register is thought to be difficult, but if the notes at that pitch do seem to respond less easily, the tongue's position is disturbing the embouchure; when the air-stream is properly directed (see Section B (ii)) it is no harder to articulate in the fundamental octave than anywhere else. Proof of this is to be heard at the end of the Scherzo in Mendelssohn's *A Midsummer Night's Dream*, when in a spectacular staccato solo, descending to the lowest C♯, the flautist pronounces over 200 syllables at the approximate speed of 9 to a second (Ex.1).

Ex. 1

The tongue's encounter with the palate should produce no extraneous noises. Spitting and explosive attacks are unnecessary, and they indicate that the air is being expelled instead of released; no break is to occur between the action of the tongue and the passage of the air between the lips.

Many flautists experience difficulty in synchronizing the tongue and the fingers, and they do not realize that this is more often due to an uncertain sense of rhythm than to weakness in technique. Making the fingers and the tongue work together is not really the problem; they must all be ordered by the rhythmic pulse of the music, so if that supremely important beat is not secure they cannot coincide. Daily practice of scales, legato and detached, is the most successful remedy for this, and for numerous faults in technique; they are all to be played slowly, and then gradually faster until the tongue and the fingers, controlled by the rhythm, become as one. All these comments concern the actual production of the flute sound, articulating the phrasing, and pointing staccato and detached notes; but many passages cannot be played fast enough without resorting to the technique which is known as double-tonguing.

When the tempo demands, two syllables are pronounced instead of the normal one, the second directing the tongue to strike another part of the mouth so that a considerably quicker articulation is obtained. The normal 't' is joined by 'k', and this double-tongued 't-k' will give the very rapid staccato which is so often needed. The 'k' articulation is obviously weaker than the more forward 't', but with patient concentration the two syllables can be made to sound even, and equal in quality.

As in single-tonguing, the double type of articulation has to be attempted slowly when it is first practised. The 't' and 'k' are *releasing* air, so it is always necessary to blow simultaneously with the actual action of the tongue, gradually increasing the speed on a single note before embarking on scales and intervals in all keys. A useful practice device reverses the order; 'k-t' as an articulation strengthens the weaker syllable, but it can only be used as an exercise, because the accent inevitably devolves upon the clearer one, which is 't'. Rapid detached triplets need three syllables. 'T-k-t', known as triple-tonguing, enables very fast passages to be played but requires concentrated practice and great perseverance. Triple-tonguing is more difficult to master because there are adjacent 't's; indeed in very rapid tempi many experienced flautists admit that they descend to the use of a triple accented version of double-tonguing, an articulation which for this purpose becomes 't-k-t, k-t-k'. This rather second-rate method is acceptable only in abnormally fast passages, and care must be taken to emphasize the 'k' when it takes its place as the principal note of the group. If a triplet is preceded by a single note of the same value it is to be articulated by a 't'; the highest standards always obtain in instrumental technique, and it will be found that the tongue can be trained to subscribe to them.

## F   Dynamics

The flute has great variety of tone colour, and a wider range of dynamics than is generally supposed. Composers have long known that it possesses dramatic qualities which can dominate an entire orchestra, and that in other moods its quieter sounds speak with the subtlest nuances; but these fascinating effects make havoc of the intonation when they are not disciplined. Pitch in crescendo and diminuendo is discussed in Section D, and it presents the main difficulty in achieving a powerful tone which can be reduced to a controlled pianissimo. Loud blowing is easy, and playing quietly too, but remaining in tune at the same time demands skill and experience. Above all, one must be conscious that intonation suffers whenever there is a change in dynamics. Lavish vibrato, the bane of much flute-playing, often stems from insecurity in these circumstances; it is in itself a distortion of the pitch, and it can destroy one of the most beautiful aspects of performance, the sensitive use of pure intervals. Natural vibrato is an integral part of resonance, and is the subject of Section B (ii) in Chapter 4; this is not to be equated with an artificial veneer that obscures real tone.

A rise in pitch is encouraged by the enlargement of the embouchure for a forte passage; using less breath in quiet playing allows it to fall; so it is necessary to combat these inherent weaknesses by adjusting the direction and strength of the air. Muscles at the corners of the mouth control the tension of the lips, the lower of which directs the stream of air, so that there is absolute command of the sound. A firm embouchure—not a forced one—is needed at all dynamic levels, but for different reasons. In forte playing when the air has to be strong and concentrated, the size of the embouchure is often reduced, and the lower lip withdrawn to keep the pitch secure; but a warmer, less intense loud sound requires a more relaxed, large embouchure and therefore still greater control of the intonation.

## (a) *Piano*

A piano dynamic requires a smaller amount of breath, and a change of embouchure to prevent an otherwise inevitable drop in pitch, especially in the two lower octaves.

Section B (iii) deals with the second register, and the position of the mouth when raising the jet of air and reducing the size of the slit between the lips. This procedure, further discussed in Section D (i), also controls the intonation in piano passages throughout the compass of the flute.

In the *lowest register* (see B (ii)) the air is now aimed at an object that is situated at the same level as the mouth; the lips hold the pitch, without allowing the second octave to materialize, and direct a small amount of air to make contact with the opposite edge of the mouth-hole. The softest sounds can be perfectly in tune, *a niente*, when this production is mastered and provided that it is governed by the ear.

Pianissimo in the *second octave* needs a firmer embouchure, because the lips are now preventing the harmonics from reverting to their fundamentals below; there will be less pressure from the diaphragm, so the air is blown a little higher still, and again the practised ear is finally in charge.

Information in Section B (iii) indicates that the *third octave* is composed of assisted harmonics, and this enables a pianissimo to be obtained with a more relaxed embouchure than in other registers. The sound at this altitude is supported by the automatically opened vent holes, the harmonics come with little effort, and the embouchure contracts to accommodate them almost of its own accord; this affords a smaller margin of inaccuracy in pitch so there is less likelihood of failure than in other octaves, but it must not be forgotten that this comparatively unstrained production depends upon a correctly blown middle register, from which the higher notes derive.

### (b) *Forte*

The *lowest register* is less susceptible to sharpness in pitch than the other octaves (see B (ii)), but students find difficulty in actually obtaining a powerful sound in this fundamental area. A remedy for this is the practice of crescendos on $Bb^1$, the most stable of the low notes. As the breath becomes stronger the corners of the mouth are drawn back so that the lips are more taut, and the air is directed in a concentrated jet at an object which is opposite, but just below, the mouth. A rich forte tone is the result, and its quality is varied by altering the tension of the lips. The identical exercise is applied to all the low notes; even $C\natural^1$ can be played very loudly when the air is blown in this way, and the supposedly wild $C\#^2$ (see B (ii)) can be given a surprisingly penetrating timbre; but on no account may the direction of the air-stream be lowered.

The *second octave* needs careful control in loud playing. There is always danger of sharpness in this area; the lips are supporting the harmonics without the assistance of the open vent-holes which add to the security of the high notes, and at the same time they must influence the quality of the tone. The technique of crescendo and diminuendo in this and the *third octave* is explained in D (i), where it is made clear that the direction of the air-stream, the strength of the breath and the tension of the lips, combine in enabling the sound to be controlled at its loudest.

# 3

# ANNOTATED FINGERING CHARTS

## A  Preferred Fingerings

Tables of fingerings for the three flute registers are provided in Section B (ii) of Chapter 2. These will enable a disciplined technique to be acquired, and they must be scrupulously adhered to until every major and minor scale has been mastered in all octaves. It is then permissible to consider the use of alternatives that are acceptable in certain circumstances. Nevertheless, two fingerings have already been allowed for a few notes:

(i) A♯ (B♭) is provided with an alternative in Charts 1 and 2 because the first is essential in chromatic passages, whereas the second is more convenient in flat keys (until the scale of G♭, which demands both B♭ and C♭) and is acoustically superior.

(ii) F♯ (G♭) is similarly endowed in all three charts, the second fingering being often necessary when it follows E♮ at speed.

(iii) G♯³: Chart 3 indicates that the second and third fingers of the right hand may be released for this note, in order to facilitate fast passages involving A♯³ (B♭³) or B♮³.

These instances indicate that acceptable alternative fingerings are in existence, but they are the only ones in normal use; they are therefore included in the main charts.

## B  Allowed Alternatives

The finest flautists rarely descend to the use of alternative fingerings except in the performance of avant-garde music,

Chart 4. Alternative fingerings (1)

● Finger down
○ Finger up
Boxed fingering indicates the difference between the alternative fingering and the normal.

| E♮1 | F♮1 (a) | F♮1 (b) | F#1 (a) | F#1 (b) | B♭1 | C#2 | D♭2 | D♮2 | D#2 | E♮2 |
|---|---|---|---|---|---|---|---|---|---|---|
| Alternating with C♮1 C#1 D♮1 | With C♮1 C#1 D♮1 | With G♮1 | With E♮1 | With C♮1 C#1 D♮1 | See chart 1 and instructions in 3A (i). | With D♮2 | With E♮2 F#2 F#2 etc. | With E♮2 F#2 F#2 etc. | With E♮2 F#2 F#2 etc. | With D#2 |
| flat | flat | flat | flat | flat | | | | | | |

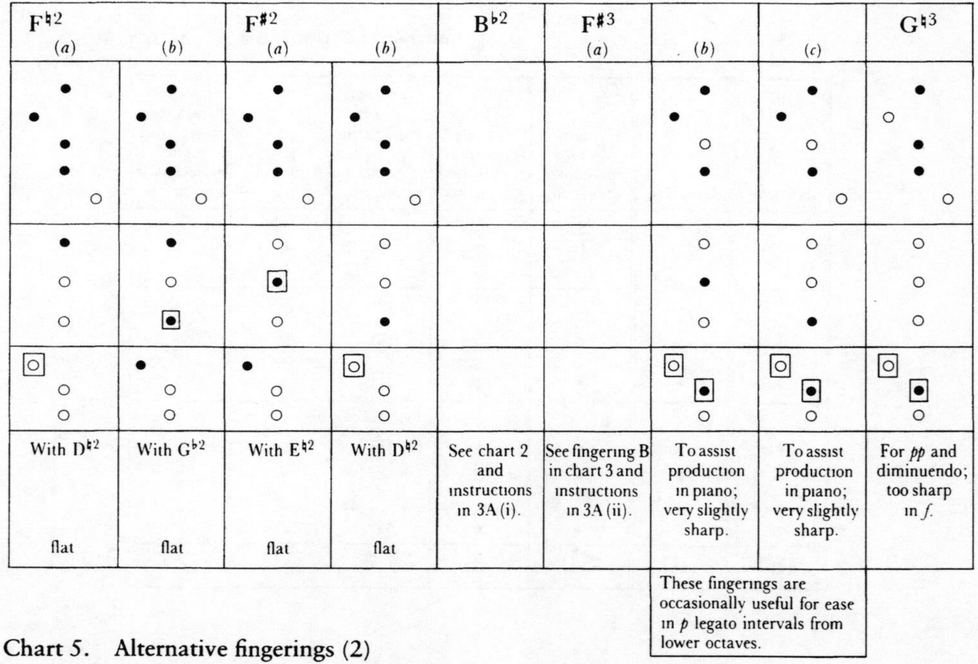
F♮2
(a)
(b)
F♯2
(a)
(b)
B♭2
F♯3
(a)
(b)
(c)
G♮3
With D♮2
With G♭2
With E♮2
With D♮2
flat
flat
flat
flat
See chart 2 and instructions in 3A (i).
See fingering B in chart 3 and instructions in 3A (ii).
To assist production in piano; very slightly sharp.
To assist production in piano; very slightly sharp.
For pp and diminuendo; too sharp in f.
These fingerings are occasionally useful for ease in p legato intervals from lower octaves.

Chart 5. Alternative fingerings (2)

| G♯3 | A♮3 | B♭3 | B♮3 | C♮4 | C♯4 | D♮4 |
|---|---|---|---|---|---|---|
| See fingering B in chart 3 and instructions in 3A (iii). | For sustaining in *pp*. | Alternating with E♭3, E♮3, F♯3. An easy but slightly sharp note. | This is used only when it is impossible to depress key ▯. | For a long piano note; slightly sharp. | Normal extra fingerings. | |

Chart 6.   Alternative fingerings (3)

and that aspect of flute-playing is dealt with in an Appendix. The original fingerings (i.e. those in Charts 1, 2, and 3) are always preferable, because they are acoustically accurate in sound and pitch; therefore every effort is made to avoid the others, unless it is impossible to negotiate a particularly difficult passage in the normal way.

Chart 4 presents some possible occasional fingerings, and the accompanying comments explain when they may be used, but also indicate their deficiences. In rare instances poaching on the preserves of the table of trills (see Section C, Charts 7–10) is permitted, but this dangerous procedure must not become habitual; each trill fingering is itself a compromise, devised to make certain ornaments possible, and is therefore usually to be reserved for its original purpose.

## C Trills

Flute music abounds in trills, and in the lower two octaves they are usually easy to play. The third register presents difficulties because several fingers are often simultaneously involved, so that such rapid ornaments become impossible. It is then necessary to resort to the special trill fingerings that are mentioned in Section B of this chapter, and which are given with comments in Charts 7–10 below; however, it is incumbent upon the flautist to practise assiduously to avoid their use whenever possible, for the reason that most of them are not truly in tune.

## D Positions of the Embouchure in the Three Registers and in the Two Breaks

Correct fingering is no guarantee of pure intonation. The subject is discussed in Chapter 2, but here it is emphasized that mastery of Charts 1, 2, and 3, and their acceptable alternatives, must be balanced by a healthy embouchure; hence some further remarks upon the direction of the air-stream, and information on dealing with sensitive areas which

| Db1–E♮1 | Eb1–F♮1 | F♮1–Gb1 | F#1–G#1 | G#1–A#1 | A♮1–Bb1 (a) (b) | Bb1–C♮2 | C♮2–Db2 | C#2–Db2 | C#2–D#2 |
|---|---|---|---|---|---|---|---|---|---|
| The D♯ key has to remain closed. | It is not possible to use fingering A for F♯ in this trill. | | | All three fingers must be involved. | Use (a) wherever possible. | Alternatives are not recommended because the C is disturbed. | Not key ♯. | Not key ♯. | Only key ♯. |

● Finger down
○ Finger up
♪ Denotes trill finger

Chart 7.  Trill fingerings (1)

| $D^{\natural2}-E^{b2}$ | $D^{\sharp2}-E^{\natural2}$ | $E^{b2}-F^{\natural2}$ | $E^{\natural2}-F^{\sharp2}$ | $F^{\natural2}-G^{b2}$ | $F^{\sharp2}-G^{\sharp2}$ | $G^{\sharp2}-A^{\natural2}$ | $A^{\natural2}-B^{b2}$ | $B^{b2}-C^{\natural3}$ | $C^{\natural3}-D^{\natural3}$ |
|---|---|---|---|---|---|---|---|---|---|
| The D♯ key has to remain closed and the 1st finger of left hand depressed. | The 1st finger of left hand remains depressed. | Both RH keys must be trilled and the 1st LH finger depressed. | See $E^{\natural1}-F^{\sharp1}$ | See $F^{\natural1}-G^{b1}$ | See $F^{\sharp1}-G^{\sharp1}$ | See $G^{\sharp1}-A^{\sharp1}$ | See $A^{\natural1}-B^{b1}$ | See $B^{b1}-C^{\natural2}$ | Not key |

Chart 8. Trill fingerings (2)

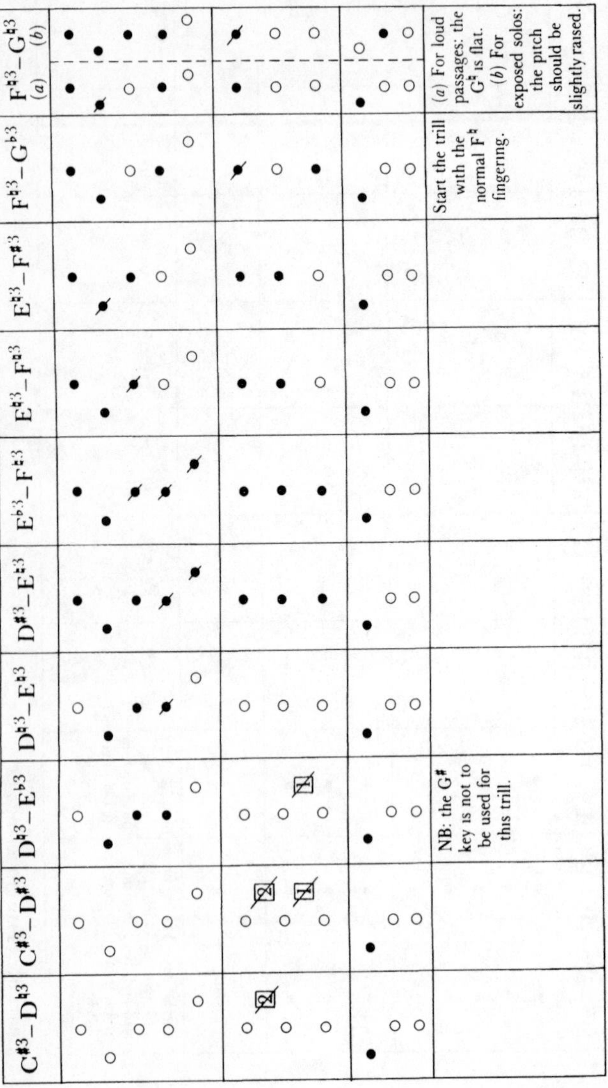


Chart 9. Trill fingerings (3)

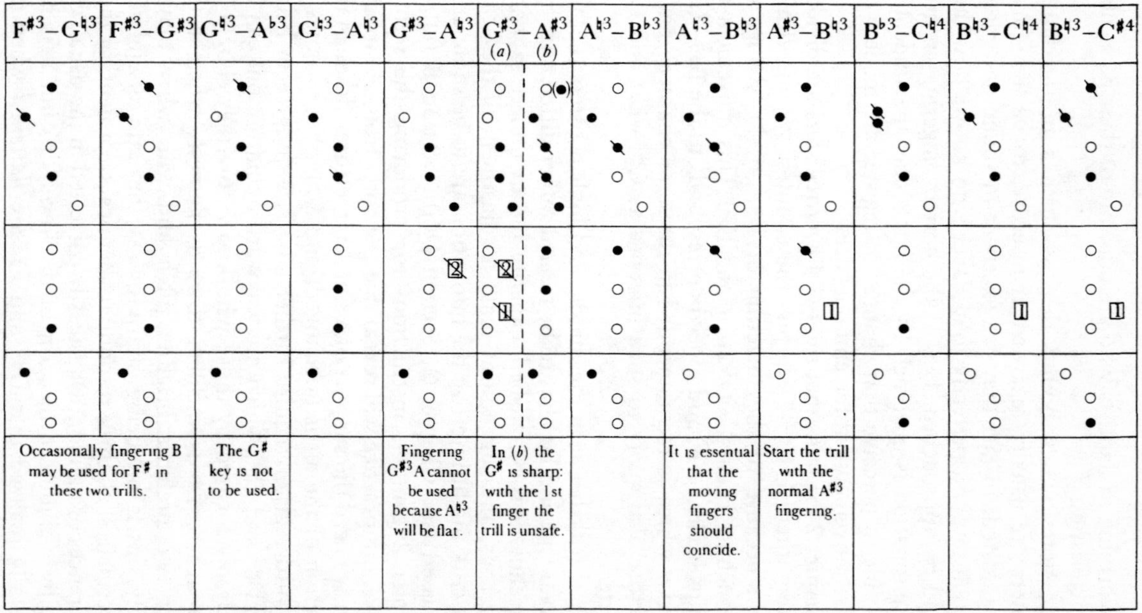


Chart 10. Trill fingerings (4)

are worrying to flautists who are unaware of their particular characteristics.

The notes which bound the two breaks in the flute's registers are usually regarded as insecure, to be humoured and adjusted; in fact they are excellent in sound and pitch, and will respond perfectly to a player who knows how they should be approached. Use of the correct fingering ensures that intonation is governed by the lips alone; the student is then able to perceive that changes of register are made with precise movements of the embouchure.

Chapter 2 explains that the two lower registers are divided by the interval $C\sharp^2$–$D\natural^2$, but these notes are identically blown because of the fingering of $D\natural$, so the change of embouchure occurs between it and $E\flat^2$. This movement of the lips is clear-cut, and indeed corresponds to the $B\flat^1$—$G\natural^2$ exercise which is recommended in the same chapter; it will therefore also apply to such intervals as $C\sharp^2$—$E\natural^2$ and $C\natural^2$ $E\flat^2$ etc.

The break between the middle and high registers (i.e. the interval $C\sharp^3$ and $D\natural^3$ has to be treated rather differently, but the technique is established; experiments are unnecessary and dangerous, and suggestions that an adjustment of the head-joint cork might improve the intonation are to be summarily dismissed (see Chapter 2, Section D(ii)). Section B (iii) in Chapter 2 contains instructions for producing the second octave, but practice will reveal that the notes from $B\flat^2$ to $C\sharp^3$ inclusive need the support of a smaller aperture, although the direction of the air is unchanged; and a number of notes in the third register require further advice, among them being $D\natural^3$, $D\sharp^3$ and $E\natural^3$, which are wayward by nature but can be admirably focused by those who know how they should be approached. $D\natural$ is inclined towards flatness, whereas the other two prefer a brighter pitch and will, when played loudly, insist on being sharp unless they are disciplined. Nevertheless, all three respond to identical treatment for their differences of opinion; $D\natural$ is easily corrected in the usual way (viz. by a minute projection of the lower lip) but it is not generally realized that $D\sharp^3$ and $E\natural^3$ are *flattened* when the same alteration is made to the embouchure. Those two notes are alone in their reaction to the raising of the air-stream, so the pitch of all three is controlled similarly and the intonation can be maintained with the most powerful sound.

F$\sharp^3$ is always insecure. The necessary vent in the left hand (see Chapter 2, Section B (iii)) can only be open in conjunction with its lower neighbour (operated by the second finger), which ought to be closed, so the note is over-vented there and under-vented in the right hand, where the third finger has to be depressed to do mechanical duty in closing another non-fingered key. Boehm, well aware of the consequences of such an arrangement (the lower F$\sharp$s are also slightly affected), has subtly organized the positions of the holes so that the intonation is undisturbed; the recommended first fingering for F$\sharp^3$ should be used, and the danger of its falling to B$\natural^2$ is avoided by the support of a firmer embouchure than is usual in the third register. (But see also Alternative Fingering Chart 5.)

G$\sharp^3$ is allocated two fingerings in Chart 3, for the purely technical reasons that are given in Chapter 3, Section A (i). The first one gives a magnificent note, so it is strange that the inferior though sometimes indispensable alternative is normally recommended; it is sharp in pitch and difficult to articulate quietly, so an introduction to its superior has often given peace of mind to experienced players who dreaded certain exposed moments in orchestral music.

# 4
## STYLE

A fine style comprises a combination of mysterious and important attributes, some of which cannot be taught or acquired. Musicians create their own personal manner of interpretation but this must not disturb the composer's intentions, and although knowledge, sensitivity, and imagination are among the prerequisites for an artist in any field, it is impossible to put them into practice without the support of secure technical control.

## A Phrasing: the Means of Controlling it

Imperfections, concealed by artificial expression, become conspicuous in genuine playing, where subtle dynamics cause lapses in intonation which alert ears and lips must prevent. A drop in pitch can ruin elegant shading at the end of a group of notes, and a crescendo that becomes sharp can do just as much damage; but the skilled player avoids such hazards by using techniques for the control of dynamics (these are explained in Chapter 2, Section F).

An example of a passage that can be dangerous for the unwary occurs in the second movement of Schubert's 'Unfinished' Symphony in B minor (Ex. 2). The simple bar is deceptively innocent in appearance, the phrasing is clearly indicated, and it seems to pose no difficulties, nevertheless after decades of playing, the writer well remembers the one occasion when he controlled it to his own satisfaction.

Ex. 2

Andante con moto

*decrescendo*

The whole bar is played very quietly, yet the first note is accented, before it immediately embarks upon a diminuendo which only ends when the pianissimo E♮ completes a perfect musical sigh. Throughout its little journey the pitch of the sound must be maintained and the temptation to play loudly resisted, so that the sensitive embouchure serves the ear and controls the phrasing.

Voluptuous sounds, with unsuitable rubato, obscure the meaning and shape of a phrase, but accuracy and respect for simplicity put no constraints on generous feelings: self-discipline cultivates a style that is original without disregard for the composer's intentions, and which can reproduce many musical voices without recourse to contrived emotions.

## B Tone

### (i) *Variety of Nuance and the Influence of Music upon it*

The greater understanding a flautist possesses, the more interesting is his sound; its quality is determined by feeling for the music, just as an orator's voice is coloured by his belief in what he says. It follows that musicianship is essential for the production of distinguished tone; realization of the direction of a phrase and sensitivity to the implications of the harmony that supports it, and is often contained within it, has a profound effect upon the perception of an artist and therefore on the sound he produces.

An actor who is obsessed with his own voice transforms every character into himself, so he is no interpreter; in a similar way, if a flautist puts tone before phrasing his playing lacks punctuation and meaning.

Intonation is at the core of tone: a pure note is achieved only by the exact focusing of the sound, an accomplishment that needs the gift of a good ear and the will to master essential embouchure techniques through the concentrated practice of scales and arpeggios—those foundations which exert such a powerful influence on both music and performance.

## (ii) *Vibrato*

Wind instruments resemble the voice, in that they possess an inherent vibrato in their natural sounds, a quality that changes character with the varying emotions of the player. As with most facets of flute technique, vibrato is the servant of the music; the paramount consideration is to restrain it from becoming obvious. Fastidious taste is offended by its extravagant use, which makes a generous contribution to the cloying style of playing that is so unworthy of this instrument.

A perpetual vibrato is to be discouraged, because its cultivation is at the expense of interpretation and destroys the true sound of the flute. Irritating to the listener and annoying to players of other instruments, it often verges on absurdity, yet only the most heartless flautist manages with none at all and it is an integral part of a fine artist's style. Excessive vibrato is a means of tawdry expression which apparently tempts flautists alone among the woodwind, and its legitimate production is not equivalent to the technique forming part of the standard training of string players.

Such a natural element of the sound cannot be acquired, and its absence is a rare phenomenon suggesting a sad lack of musicality; only a pronounced vibrato should encourage discussion of the subject, and then it should be emphasized that it never involves the lips because their movement influences the pitch; its production is essentially controlled by air pressure from the lungs, as it is with the voice. No singer ought to learn to use vibrato: a fine one ensures that it never obtrudes. (See also Chapter 2, Section F.)

# 5

# THE PRACTICE OF SCALES, ARPEGGIOS, AND EXERCISES

## (i) *For the Embouchure*

The daily discipline of practising scales in all major and minor keys has always been regarded as the most successful way to obtain an assured and reliable instrumental technique. In flute-playing the ear, lips, and fingers are trained so that the whole range of sound is played in tune and in time, fast and slow, at all dynamic levels. The function of the embouchure is to produce the various registers and simultaneously control the intonation, a task that becomes almost unconscious if it is correctly approached. At an early stage the scales are practised mezzo-forte and slowly, avoiding the crescendo and diminuendo that are so inviting, so that the lips adjust themselves at precisely the right moment for the first note in a different octave. The information in Chapters 2 (Section B (ii) and (iii)) and 3 (Section D) explains that neglect of the correct embouchure positions leads to an imperfect control of the sound, whereas careful attention to those directions results in a natural command of the pitch at any tempo.

Experienced flautists are able to forget what their lips are doing and concentrate on the music, until a rest from practising reminds them that the skill is temporary, but perpetual stimulation can stem from the knowledge that Practice never does Make Perfect. Chapter 2 contains advice on playing scales in piano and forte, with or without crescendo and diminuendo, and during these regular exercises the ear must constantly criticize the results. True pitch is indispensable for the production of free tone, so impure intonation causes a false sound that has to be put in focus; scale practice remains the ideal way to observe and eradicate one's own faults.

Arpeggios are approached in a similar way to scales, except that the lips need more frequent adjustments to cope with the continual changing of octaves. Practice soon makes the embouchure accustomed to the necessary movements and the result will be a noticeable ease of production, providing confidence and removing much of the strain that is associated with inadequate technical equipment.

## (ii) *For the Fingers and Tongue*

Scales are to be played legato and staccato in STRICT TIME, with natural accents on appropriate beats in the bar— hurrying is a sign of weakness, although dragging does not necessarily indicate strength. Determined flautists discover an infinite number of permutations in grouping the notes for this purpose: legato scales are practised in one long slur, or divided into shorter phrases; tongued ones can be entirely staccato or a combination of both; and every form of tonguing (single, double, and triple, depending on the speed and rhythm) must be incorporated in these self-organized studies, which are similarly applicable to arpeggios in all keys.

Difficulty can be experienced in persuading the fingers and tongue to coincide: scale practice is an excellent remedy for this weakness, and it should be used systematically after consulting Chapter 2, Section E. The following rules will help to forestall bad habits in fingering and tonguing:

1. Every finger must rest on the centre of each key.
2. The right-hand thumb supports the flute, underneath the tube and immediately below the first finger; if it slips forward, the hand leaves its correct position on the keys.
3. The left-hand thumb is placed ON ITS SIDE, between the B♮ and B♭ levers, so that it *turns*, not slides, from one to the other; the fingers will then fall comfortably on to the centre, and not the edge, of the keys. The mechanism is arranged to accommodate the hand in this position.
4. Adherence to the fingerings in Charts 1, 2, and 3 is essential; no alternatives may be used until all the exercises

can be confidently played. Refer to Chapter 3, Section A (i) for A♯ (B♭) fingerings. It is important to note that there is to be no relaxation of the rule that the D♯ key is open for E♮s, and closed for the highest B♭, B♮ and C♮; care must also be taken always to *raise the first left-hand finger* for D♮² and D♯².

5. Concentration on fingering in these exercises can lead to carelessness in the proper action of the tongue, with the result that articulation is blurred and the embouchure is disturbed. Chapter 2, Section E deals with the subject; and scale exercises provide a regular means of making certain that the tongue is being used healthily.

6. Scales and arpeggios are to be played with beauty, never mechanically; they form the basis of all music and should be regarded with equal respect. The sensitive repetition of these shapely phrases relaxes the tongue and the fingers so that they are responsive, and free of the tension that sometimes restricts their movements; single-tonguing is made easier, and the uncomfortable gap between it and the double and triple speeds is eliminated.

7. The recommended cycle of exercises contains:

> Major scales
> Minor scales (harmonic and melodic forms)
> Chromatic scales
> Arpeggios of common chords (major and minor, and inversions)
> Arpeggios of dominant and diminished sevenths (and inversions)

To be played in all keys, legato and staccato, piano and forte.

# 6

# THE TECHNIQUE OF
# ORCHESTRAL PLAYING

The orchestra provides magnificent opportunities for the flute but great responsibilities for the player, who is required to be a soloist in his own right, a chamber musician, and to have the stamina and confidence to dominate in tutti passages when the occasion arises. Its very position on the crest of the score gives the flautist a dangerous opportunity to make or mar the quality of a performance, an exposure that needs constant self-appraisal.

The most noticeable blemish among flautists in these circumstances is a persistent fluttering, sometimes frenzied, vibrato which is usually sharp in pitch and bears no relation to the style of the music or the conventional sounds of the other woodwind. The discipline of chamber music presents an ideal way to counteract such faults, and it thus contributes a great deal to the training of a symphonic player: small ensembles have to be sensitive to the slightest nuance in tone and pitch in their pursuit of a perfect blend of ideas, and familiarity with colleagues and their manner of exchanging phrases in music is a pleasure that raises and maintains standards; orchestral playing demands a similar but wider approach. The woodwind choir is surrounded by strings, brass, and percussion, with which its members collaborate individually and as a group, and one instrument can upset the intonation and balance of the whole; it is not always easy to identify the weak spot, so an assured technique needs flexibility and sympathy with colleagues' problems. Knowledge of the distinctive characteristics of other instruments is desirable, but appreciation of one's own failings is essential.

In orchestral playing there is a difference between absolute solos, and exposed passages in the ensemble. In the spacious centre-piece of Ravel's Second Suite from *Daphnis et Chloë*, a celebrated *tour de force* for the flute, the wisest conductors follow the player and concentrate on the accompaniment; on the other hand he is a foolish maestro who refrains from suggesting the tempo of the unaccompanied opening phrase of Debussy's *Prélude à l'après-midi d'un faune*, because although the flautist sets the scene, the interpretation of the whole piece is not his responsibility. There are also many short individual passages that are the flautist's own; an example is the dramatic response to the horn call in the introduction to the last movement of Brahms's First Symphony—the flute's proudest contribution to the work, and one of its great symphonic challenges. The orchestral woodwind soloists cannot always give such rein to their feelings: as members of a close-knit group of artists they all have their say, but also have the opportunity to respond or give place to each other when the music dictates. This aspect of playing needs a technique that only experience can acquire, but knowledge of the problems and how to solve them provide the best introduction to it. Intonation is always a worry for wind players in the midst of an orchestra, so the ear must constantly be on the alert to correct the pitch or adapt it to accommodate others. Listening should be (*a*) horizontal—melodic phrases with other instruments can be in unison, octaves, thirds, and indeed at every interval; and (*b*) vertical—each instrument is also used as part of the harmony, and when the flute is at the top its pitch must be influenced by the whole chord.

Notes often need a minute adjustment to make the intonation pure, just as a small change of dynamic can immediately correct an imbalance. The higher the standard of performance the more necessary is the ability to play quietly: the novice symphonic flautist is usually dismayed to discover that this applies to the largest orchestras, and it is a shock that a pianissimo can have disastrous consequences if its pitch is not under control.

Audiences enjoy watching conductors and are sometimes disappointed when there is little to be seen. Flamboyant gestures disturb the orchestra, and the resultant unsteady rhythm annoys professional players; those who are not so confident are confused, they blame themselves and in their innocence are often impressed, but the clear beat of a real master inspires musicians of every calibre to reach heights that only powerful simplicity can govern. However, between the plainly indicated bar-lines there has to be accuracy; strict adherence to note values is essential for ensemble, in spite of the slight expressive rubato of distinguished interpretations, so orchestral players do not indulge in the excesses of the uncultivated.

Careless regard for apparently ordinary rhythms is the normal reason for poor ensemble; among common examples is ♫, rendered as ♩♪ or ♪♫, but rarely correctly; another sufferer is ♫♫, whose deformity is ♪♫ or ♩♫; triplets are often ♫♩ or ♩♫, and these are only a few of the numerous distortions that must be recognized and eschewed by all musicians, but which cause chaos in chamber and orchestral music. It is impossible for a number of people to play groups of notes perfectly together if the values are incorrect; inaccuracy creates trouble and wastes rehearsal time, so artists school themselves to be scrupulously exact.

Clean articulation is *de rigueur* in polite woodwind society and nowhere more so than in the orchestra. Oboists and bassoonists have exemplary manners because it is difficult for them to start a note without using the tongue, whereas flautists and clarinettists can dispense with it only too easily; a blurred attack brings unstable pitch, poor sounds, and unbalanced dynamics.

A player who habitually articulates clearly, with correct embouchure and fingering, has the confidence to concentrate on phrasing and the subtle shades in dynamics that exist in symphonic music. The composer's instructions MUST be obeyed by every player; when they are ignored, accompanying parts stand out, important passages are drowned, and nonsense is made of a carefully orchestrated score.

# 7

# REPERTOIRE

The flute repertoire is large, so the following list contains only works of essential interest. Excellent minor composers of the Baroque Era produced much pleasant solo and ensemble music which has no great individuality or unusual beauty; there are important exceptions, but most of the compositions are useful for musical evenings without being indispensable to the serious student, although he would wish to add many of them to his library in due course. C. P. E. Bach and his brothers; Quantz and Frederick the Great; Telemann and his contemporaries; all these composed elegant works in the style of the time, but none can challenge the outstanding flute music of J. S. Bach and Handel, the two greatest musicians of the early eighteenth century.

Bach provided magnificent concertante parts in his second orchestral suite and Fifth Brandenburg Concerto, superb and taxing obbligatos in the Passions and Cantatas, and among his splendid flute sonatas the B minor is possibly the finest of all compositions in that genre.

Handel's beautiful collection, although more simple in style than Bach's, remains a salutary reminder of our own unworthiness as his interpreters. Some decades later there appeared Mozart's two famous concertos, his double one with harp, an Andante with orchestra, and four quartets with strings. The quartet in D major (K. 285), one of his best small chamber works, contains a slow movement of rare beauty; surely only Gluck in Orfeo and Brahms in the Passacaglia of his Fourth Symphony have so wonderfully evoked the flute's unique quality of noble serenity.

There is no solo music by Beethoven, but his spectacular Serenade (Op. 25) for flute, violin, and viola is a gem which lasts some 25 minutes, and puts all three players to the test in technique and musicianship.

In the nineteenth century enthusiastic amateurs were eager to add to their repertoires, and they were indulged by the fashionable flautist-composers of the day, whose effusions usually gave more pleasure to devotees of the flute than to those of music. The most successful of the more serious of these composers, Friedrich Kuhlau, produced numerous Grand Sonatas, duets, trios, and even a good quartet for flutes, but the quality of the solo repertoire still remained indifferent until leading orchestral composers became aware of the instrument's many capabilities, and were inspired to create music which would reflect them.

Much excellent flute music has appeared in Europe and America during the present century; this list comprises some of the most important pieces from all periods, except the now extensive *oeuvre* of the avant-garde composers. A comprehensive catalogue of flute music has been compiled by the Dutch flautist Frans Vester; his volume, embracing practically every printed work, and many that are in manuscript, is published by Musica Rara.

# A   Solo Music

ALWYN, WILLIAM (1905–84), *Divertimento* (unaccompanied) (Boosey and Hawkes).

ARNOLD, MALCOLM (1921–  ), Concerto No. 1 (Patterson).

—— Concerto No. 2 (Faber).

—— Sonatina (Lengnick).

—— *Fantasy* (unaccompanied) (Faber).

ARRIEU, CLAUDE (1903–  ), Sonatine (Amphion).

BACH, CARL PHILIPP EMMANUEL (1714–88), Sonata in A minor (unaccompanied) (Zimmermann).

—— Many sonatas with continuo (various publishers).

BACH, JOHANN SEBASTIAN (1685–1750), Six sonatas (Peters); B minor, E flat major, A major for flute and obbligato cembalo; C major, E minor, E major for flute and continuo.

—— Partita in A minor (unaccompanied) (Bärenreiter).

—— Sonata in G minor for flute and obbligato cembalo (Leduc).

BERIO, LUCIANO (1925– ), *Sequenza* (unaccompanied) (Zerboni).

BERKELEY, LENNOX (1903–89), Concerto (Chester).

—— Sonatina (Schott).

BLAVET, MICHEL (1700–68), Many sonatas with continuo (various publishers).

BOULEZ, PIERRE (1925– ), Sonatine (Amphion).

BOWEN, YORK (1884–1961), Sonata (Emerson).

BUSONI, FERUCCIO (1866–1924), *Divertimento* with orchestra; and with piano arrangement by KURT WEILL under the supervision of the composer (Breitkopf and Härtel).

CASELLA, ALFREDO (1883–1947), *Barcarola* and *Scherzo* (Salabert).

—— *Sicilienne* and *Burlesque* (Leduc).

CHAMINADE, CÉCILE (1857–1944), *Concertino* (with orchestra or piano) (Enoch).

CIMAROSA, DOMENICO (1749–1801), *Concertante* for 2 flutes and orchestra (Bote and Bock).

DEBUSSY, CLAUDE (1862–1918), *Syrinx* (unaccompanied) (Jobert).

DUKAS, PAUL (1865–1935), *Alla Gitana* (Leduc).

DUTILLEUX, HENRI (1916– ), Sonatine (Leduc).

ENESCO, GEORGES (1881–1955), *Cantabile et presto* (Enoch).

FAURÉ, GABRIEL (1845–1924), *Fantaisie* (Hamelle).

—— *Pièce* (Leduc).

—— *Morceau de Concours* (Bourne).

FRANÇAIX, JEAN (1912– ), *Divertimento* (Schott).

—— Suite (unaccompanied) (Schott).

FUKISHIMA, KASUO (1930– ), *Mei* (Zerboni).

GAUBERT, PHILIPPE (1879–1941), *Nocturne* and *Allegro Scherzando* (Enoch).

—— Sonatine (Hengel).

—— (and many other pieces).

GERHARD, ROBERTO (1896–1970), *Capriccio* (unaccompanied) (Mills).

GHEDINI, GEORGIO (1892–1965), *Sonata da Concerto* with orchestra (Ricordi).

GLUCK, CHRISTOPH VON (1714–87), Concerto (Hug).

GODARD, BENJAMIN (1849–95), Suite with orchestra or piano (Durand).

GOEHR, ALEXANDER (1932– ), *Variations* (Schott).

GRÊTRY, ANDRÉ (1741–1813), Concerto (Andraud).

HAHN, REYNALDO (1875–1947), *L'Enchanteur* (Hengel).

HANDEL, GEORGE FREDERIC (1685–1759), Sonatas (Peters).

HINDEMITH, PAUL (1895–1963), Sonata (Schott).

—— *Echo* (Schott).

—— *Acht Stücke* (Schott).

—— *Kanonische Sonatine* (2 flutes alone) (Schott).

HONEGGER, ARTHUR (1892–1955), *Danse de la Chèvre* (unaccompanied) (Salabert).

—— *Concerto da Camera* (flute, cor anglais, and strings) (Salabert).

HOTTETERRE, JACQUES (1650–1738), *Echos* (unaccompanied) (Schott).

HÜE, GEORGES (1858–1948), *Fantaisie* (Leduc).

IBERT, JACQUES (1890–1962), Concerto (Leduc).

—— *Jeux* (Sonatine) (Leduc).

—— *Pièce pour flûte seule* (Leduc).

JACOB, GORDON (1895–1984), Concerto (Stainer and Bell).

JOLIVET, ANDRÉ (1905–74), Concerto (Hengel).

—— *Chant de Linos* (Leduc).

—— *Cinq Incantations* (unaccompanied) (Boosey and Hawkes).

KOECHLIN, CHARLES (1867–1951), Sonata (Salabert).

—— *14 Petites Pièces* (Salabert).

—— 3 Sonatines (unaccompanied) (Salabert).

—— Sonata (2 flutes alone) (Salabert).

KUHLAU, FRIEDRICH (1786–1832), Numerous works (Peters etc.).

LECLAIR, JEAN MARIE (1697–1764), Sonatas (International Music Co.).

LOCATELLI, PIETRO (1695–1764), Sonatas (Bärenreiter).

LOEILLET, JEAN BAPTISTE (1680–1730), Sonatas (Bärenreiter).

MARTIN, FRANK (1890–1974), *Ballade* (Universal).

—— *Sonata da Chiesa* (with organ) (Universal).

MARTINŮ, BOHUSLAV (1890–1959), Sonata (Associated Music Publishers).

MERCADENTE, SAVERIO (1795–1870), Concerto (Zerboni).

MESSAIEN, OLIVIER (1908–  ), *Le merle noir* (Leduc).

MILHAUD, DARIUS (1892–1974), Sonatine (Durand).

MOZART, WOLFGANG AMADEUS (1756–91), Concerto in G major, K. 313 (Breitkopf and Härtel).

—— Concerto in D major, K. 314 (Breitkopf and Härtel).

—— Andante in C major, K. 315 (with orchestra) (Breitkopf and Härtel).

—— Concerto (with harp and orchestra), K. 299 (Breitkopf and Härtel).

NIELSEN, CARL (1865–1931), Concerto (Samfundit).

PIERNÉ PAUL (1874–1952), *Aubade* (Leduc).

PISTON, WALTER (1894–1976), Sonata (Coss Cobb).

POULENC, FRANCIS (1899–1963), Sonata (Chester).

PROKOFIEV, SERGEI (1891–1954), Sonata (Sikorski).

QUANTZ, JOHANN JOACHIM (1697–1773), Concertos and Sonatas (various publishers).

RAWSTHORNE, ALAN (1905–71), *Concertante Pastorale* for flute, horn, and orchestra (Oxford University Press).

REINECKE, KARL (1824–1910), Sonata ('Undine') (International Music Co.).

REIZENSTEIN, FRANZ (1911–68), *Partita* (Schott).

ROPARTZ, GUY (1864–1955), Sonatine (Leduc).

ROUSSEL, ALBERT (1869–1937), *Aria (Leduc)*.

—— *Joueurs de Flûte* (4 pieces) (Durand).

—— *Andante et Scherzo* (Durand).

SAINT-SAËNS, Camille (1835–1921), *Romance* (Durand).

SCHERS, SIGNOR (*fl.* 1740), 6 Sonatas (Hug).

SCHUBERT, FRANZ (1797–1828), *Introduction, Theme and Variations* (Peters).

SCHULOFF, ERWIN (1894–1942), Sonata (Chester).

SEIBER, MATYAS (1905–60), *Pastorale and Burleske* with orchestra or piano (Schott).

STANLEY, JOHN (1713–86), Solos (sonatas) (Oxford University Press).

TELEMANN, GEORG PHILIPP (1681–1767), Concertos and Sonatas (various publishers).

—— 12 Fantasies (unaccompanied) (Bärenreiter).

—— 6 Sonatas in Canon (2 flutes alone) (International Music Co.).

VARÈSE EDGAR (1885–1965), *Density 21.5* (Ricordi).

VINCI, LEONARDO (1690–1732), Sonata in D major (Oxford University Press).

VIVALDI, ANTONIO (1675–1743), Sonatas and Concertos (various publishers).

—— Three concertos for piccolo and orchestra (Ricordi).

WELLESZ, EGON (1885–1974), Suite (unaccompanied) (Rongwen).

WIDOR, CHARLES MARIE (1845–1937), Suite (Hengel).


# B   Chamber Music

Chamber music provides the flautist with opportunities to play in a variety of combinations, the most popular of which is probably the wind quintet, but there are certain important compositions in which the flute is heard to greater advantage by being the lone wind instrument in the ensemble. The following list suggests some of the most distinguished of these works; every serious player should be familiar with such outstanding examples of the use of the instrument by composers in many styles and periods.


BACH, JOHANN SEBASTIAN (1685–1750), Sonata in C minor for flute, violin, and continuo from *The Musical Offering* (Peters).

—— Sonata in G major for flute, violin, and continuo (Peters).

—— Sonata in G major for two flutes and continuo (Peters).

BAX, ARNOLD (1883–1953), *Elegiac Trio* for flute, viola, and harp (Chester).

BEETHOVEN, LUDWIG VAN (1770–1827), Serenade in D major (Op. 25) for flute, violin, and viola (Peters).

Debussy, Claude (1862–1918), Sonata for flute, viola, and harp (Durand).

Martinů, Bohuslav (1890–1959), *Madrigal Sonata* for flute, cello, and piano (Associated Music Publishers).

Mozart, Wolfgang Amadeus (1756–91), Quartet for flute and strings in D major (K. 285) (Breitkopf and Härtel).

—— Quartet for flute and strings in A major (K. 298) (Breitkopf and Härtel).

Pierné, Gabriel (1863–1937), Sonata da Camera for flute, cello, and piano (Durand).

Piston, Walter (1894–1976), Quintet for flute and strings (Arrow).

Roussel, Albert (1869–1937), Trio for flute, viola, and cello (Durand).

—— Serenade for flute, violin, viola, cello, and harp (Durand).

Weber, Carl Maria von (1786–1826), Trio for flute, cello, and piano (Peters).

There are excellent Quintets for flute, oboe, clarinet, bassoon, and horn by the following composers:

Arnold, Malcolm (1921– )
Barber, Samuel (1910– )
Castérède, Jacques (1926– )
Damase, Jean Michel (1928– )
Danzi, Franz (1763–1826)
Françaix, Jean (1912– )
Fricker, Peter Racine (1920–90)
Gerhard, Roberto (1896–1970)
Hindemith, Paul (1895–1963)
Ibert, Jacques (1890–1962)
Ligeti, György (1923– )
Malipiero, Gian Francesco (1882–1973)
Milhaud, Darius (1892–1974)
Nielsen, Carl (1865–1931)
Reicha, Anton (1770–1836)
Seiber, Matyas (1905–60)

# C   Studies

Some flute studies are so dull and pompously difficult that they actually impede progress instead of providing interesting challenges which will lead to a fluent and controlled technique. The following short selection from the hosts of available volumes provides some hundreds of excellent études which can be of inestimable benefit in daily practice.

ALTÈS, HENRI (1826–1899), *26 Selected Studies* (Schirmer).

BOEHM, THEOBALD (1794–1881), *24 Études* (Leduc).

CASTÉRÈDE, JACQUES (1926–  ), *12 Études* (Leduc).

DROUET, LOUIS (1792–1873), *25 Études célèbres* (Leduc).

KARG-ELERT, SIEGFRIED (1879–1933), *30 Studies*, Op. 107 (International Music Co.).

KÖHLER, ERNESTO (1849–1907), *The Flautist's Progress*, Op. 33 (Zimmermann).

SCHINDLER, FRITZ (ed.), *Bachstudien* (Breitkopf and Härtel).

TAFFANEL, PAUL (1844–1908) and GAUBERT, PHILIPPE (1879–1941), *17 Grands Exercices journaliers de méchanisme* (Leduc).

VESTER, FRANS (1922–87), (ed.), *125 Classical Studies* (Universal).

—— *100 Classical Studies* (Universal).

—— *50 Classical Studies* (Universal).

VIVIAN, A. P. (1855–1903), *Scale Exercises* (Boosey and Hawkes).

# AVANT-GARDE TECHNIQUES

*Sebastian Bell*

The purpose of this appendix is to introduce certain techniques specifically associated with the twentieth century.

It would be as well to consider some points in general at this stage since musical language has developed quite quickly after the radical changes that took place around the turn of the century. When confronted by unfamiliar aspects of this language the interpreter should use common sense and musicianship when unravelling problems set by a composer who is writing down instructions in a limited notation which may have to be adapted or, in some cases, extended. For example:

## Dynamics

It is quite usual to encounter a dynamic range which runs from *pppp* to *ffff*. This enables the composer to lay down a much more precise dynamic structure but can easily be misinterpreted by the player. It should be clear that the flute has dynamic limits which are not going to be extended by more demanding instructions. To put it crudely, do not overblow when you see *ffff* on the copy.

## Accidentals

Where music is not written in a system of keys the conventions relating to accidentals will change. It cannot be assumed that accidentals will hold through the bar, nor can it be assumed that they do not.

There are various possible systems. In that used by the composers of the Second Viennese School every note requires an accidental before it: for example, to notate 4 middle Cs, with the first a sharp and the others natural, it is necessary to prefix the first note with a sharp and the remaining three each with a natural symbol. In a second system, used in the 1970s by such composers as Henze and Birtwistle, a note was assumed to be natural if it carried no preceding sharp or flat: thus to notate the Cs as above the only accidental required is the first sharp.

Less extreme conventions exist: for example, accidentals do not hold through the bar unless a note is repeated; or accidentals hold through a ligature or beam but not through the whole bar (this can be confusing, however, if a ligature extends across a bar-line).

In short, no assumptions can be made with accidentals and a bit of research with the score is often necessary.

## Space Time Notation

A system of rhythmic notation where pitches are written proportionately in a known time space, e.g. 3 cm = 4 seconds. The player has to judge their spacing and/or duration by eye. Therefore, a sustained pitch notated

would last 5 seconds. A single dot would indicate a short note. Dots close together would be fast and dots well spaced would be short notes played slowly. The usual notation for sustained sound is a line of a specific length.

## Style

Do not seek to superimpose a romantic or classical 'line' on music that has been written in modules or units. It won't work. Perhaps the clearest simile to offer players embarking on unfamiliar music is to suggest that it is thought of as a foreign tongue. The sounds may be odd, even to the extent of appearing hostile, but the sense and purpose is there and sympathetic work by the player will produce its reward.

The following examples are of necessity very brief but it is hoped that they will give a working introduction to the extended sounds most frequently required.

## Soufflé Air Sound

No actual note, just a hint of pitch from the given fingering. Use a lot of air but direct it in such a way that the flute does not sound.

## Harmonics

Usually notated when alternative sound is required. Use natural harmonic fingering (Fundamental) or corrected fingering (Fundamental + Vent).

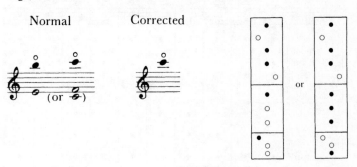

## Double Harmonics

Obtained off natural fundamentals. Great dexterity in lip control required.

## Multiphonics

Obtained by fingering a pitch and venting a 'foreign' pitch to set up two or more simultaneous harmonic series in the tube. There are nearly 2,000 multiphonic sounds available; these are listed in various specialist publications. (T. Howell, *The Avant-Garde Flute*, University of California Press, 1974; Robert Dick, *The Other Flute*, Oxford University Press, London, 1975.)

It is advisable to learn a repertoire of twenty or so multiphonics, thereby having the ability to produce something close to a composer's intention without recourse to the guide book.

| | | | | | | | | | | | |
|---|---|---|---|---|---|---|---|---|---|---|---|
| **LEFT HAND** | 1st | ● | ● | ● | ● | ● | ● | ○ | ● | ○ | ● |
| | Thumb | ● | ● | ● | ● | ● | ○ | ● | ○ | ●● | ● |
| | 2nd | ● | ● | ● | ⊘ | ● | ● | ● | ● | ○ | ● |
| | 3rd | ● | ● | ● | ● | ● | ○ | ● | ● | ● | ● |
| | 4th | ○ | ○ | ○ | ● | ○ | ○ | ○ | ○ | ○ | ○ |
| **RIGHT HAND** | 1st | ● | ● | ○ | ● | ● | ○ | ○ | ● | ○ | ○ |
| | 2nd | ● | ○ | ● | ● | ● | ● | ○ | ● | ● | ○ |
| | 3rd | ● | ● | ● | ● | ○ | ● | ○ | ○ | ○ | □ |
| | 4th | ○ | ○ | ○ | ● | ● | ● | ● | ○ | ○ | ● |
| | | ○ | ○ | ○ | ○ | ○ | ○ | ○ | ○ | ○ | ○ |
| | | ● | ● | ● | ○ | ○ | ○ | ○ | ● | ● | ○ |

✦ = ½♯ = ¼ tone high
♩ = ½♭ = ¼ tone low
♯♯ = ¾♯ = ¼ tone higher than ♯
⊘ = Ring (French system only)

## Air Harmonics

A sound produced by covering the lip plate with the mouth, half-covering the embouchure hole with the tongue and adjusting the air-stream to produce high residual sounds. Usually notated two octaves below desired pitch.

## Whistle Tones

Very high-pitched sounds produced by making the embouchure into a large **O** and setting up eddy currents in the embouchure hole of the flute. Notated ⌇⌇⌇

## Jet Whistle

Air sound produced by covering the blow hole with the mouth and blowing vigorously. Sometimes used, unfortunately, as part of the warming up process.

## Flutter Tongue

A broken sound produced by tongue vibration as in **Thrrree**, or guttural **Frrrench** (rolled).

Notated ♪ or *Flatt.* ♪ or ♪

## Ribattimento

Very rapid, gentle double tongue. Sounds similar to soft flutter tongue.

Notated ♪

## Tremolo

Rapid alternation of two fingerings of closely similar pitch.

## Alternative Fingerings

Used to produce microtonal differences and changes of timbre.

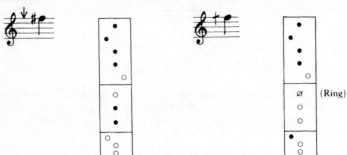

## Finger Tap/Key Slap

Use of one or more fingers to produce a percussive start to a note. G-A key is the most useful for this technique. This technique should be used sparingly, as it is not good for the pads.
Notated ✛

## Voice

It is relatively easy to sing and play at the same time and can be beneficial to the production of a good sound.

## Circular Breathing

Glassblowers' technique. A continuous airstream is maintained by using the cheeks as bellows. Having extended the cheeks to their fullest extent the player then shuts the back of the throat and breathes through the nose. Not easy on the flute because of the large volume of air required. See Robert Dick, *Circular Breathing for Flautists* (Multiple Breath Music Co., New York, 1988.)

# BIBLIOGRAPHY

BAINES, ANTHONY, *Woodwind Instruments and their History* (Faber, London, 1957).

BATE, PHILIP, *The Flute, A Study of its History, Development and Construction* (Benn, London, 1975).

BOEHM, THEOBALD, *The Flute and Flute Playing (1871)* (Dover, New York, 1964).

DICK, ROBERT, *The Other Flute* (Oxford University Press, London, 1975).

—— *Circular Breathing for Flautists* (Multiple Breath Music Co., New York, 1988).

FITZGIBBON, H. MACAULAY, *The Story of the Flute* (Reeves, London, 1928).

HOTTETERRE, JACQUES-MARTIN, *Principes de la Flûte (1707)*, trans. P. M. Douglas (Dover, New York, 1983).

HOWELL, THOMAS, *The Avant-Garde Flute* (University of California Press, Berkeley, CA, 1974).

PELLERITE, JAMES, *A Handbook of Literature for the Flute* (Zalo Publications, Bloomington, Ind., 1978).

QUANTZ, JOHANN JOACHIM, *On Playing the Flute (1752)* (Faber, London, 1966).

ROCKSTRO, RICHARD, *A Treatise on the Flute (1890)* (Musica Rara, London, 1967).

VESTER, FRANS, *Flute Repertoire Catalogue* (Musica Rara, London, 1967).